LIFE'S LITTLE INSTRUCTION BOOK

511 Reminders for a Happy and Rewarding Life

H. JACKSON BROWN, Jr.

Rutledge Hill Press
Nashville, Tennessee

Published in Nashville, Tennessee, by Rutledge Hill Press, Inc..
513 Third Avenue South, Nashville, Tennessee 37210.

Typography by Bailey Typography, Nashville, Tennessee

Library of Congress Cataloging-in-Publication Data

Brown, H. Jackson, 1940–
    Life's little instruction book / by H. Jackson Brown, Jr.
      p.   cm.
    ISBN 1-55853-121-1
    1. Happiness—Quotations, maxims, etc.   2. Conduct of life—
Quotations, maxims, etc.   I. Title.
BJ1481.B87   1991   91-9800
170′.44—dc20   CIP

Printed in the United States of America
5 6 7 8 9 10 11 — 94 93 92

Introduction

THIS BOOK began as a gift to my son, Adam. As he packed his stereo, typewriter, blue blazer and other necessities for his new life as a college freshman, I retreated to the family room to jot down a few observations and words of counsel I thought he might find useful.

I read years ago that it was not the responsibility of parents to pave the road for their children, but to provide a road map. That's how I hoped he would use these mind and heart reflections.

I started writing, and what I thought would take a few hours took several days. I gathered my collection of handwritten notes, typed them up, and put them in a dime-store binder. I walked to the garage and slid it under the front seat of the station wagon.

A few days later his mother and I helped him move into his new dorm room. When he was all settled in, I asked him to come with me to the parking lot. It was time for the presentation. I reached under the car seat and, with words to the effect that this was what I knew about living a happy and rewarding life, handed him the bound pages. He hugged me and shook my hand. It was a very special moment.

Well, somehow those typewritten pages became the little book you're now holding. You may not agree with all the entries, and from your own life experience, I'm sure you could add hundreds more. Obviously, some are more important than others, but all have added a degree of joy, meaning, and efficiency to my life.

A few days after I had given Adam his copy, he called me from his dorm room. "Dad," he said, "I've been reading the instruction book and I think it's one of the best gifts I've ever received. I'm going to add to it and someday give it to my son."

Every once in a while life hands you a moment so precious, so overwhelming you almost glow. I know. I had just experienced one.

Other books by H. Jackson Brown, Jr.:

A Father's Book of Wisdom
P.S. I Love You
Live and Learn and Pass It On

*For Adam, my son
and in many ways my teacher.*

Son, how can I help you see?
May I give you my shoulders
  to stand on?
Now you see farther than me.
Now you see for both of us.
Won't you tell me what you see?

· 1 ·

Compliment three people every day.

· 2 ·

Have a dog.

· 3 ·

Watch a sunrise at least once a year.

· 4 ·

Remember other people's birthdays.

· 5 ·

Overtip breakfast waitresses.

· 6 ·

Have a firm handshake.

· 7 ·

Look people in the eye.

· 8 ·

Say "thank you" a lot.

· 9 ·

Say "please" a lot.

· 10 ·

Learn to play a musical instrument.

· 11 ·

Sing in the shower.

· 12 ·

Use the good silver.

· 13 ·

Learn to make great chili.

· 14 ·

Plant flowers every spring.

· 15 ·

Own a great stereo system.

· 16 ·

Be the first to say, "Hello."

· 17 ·

Live beneath your means.

· 18 ·

Drive inexpensive cars,
but own the best house you can afford.

· 19 ·

Buy great books even if you never read them.

· 20 ·

Be forgiving of yourself and others.

· 21 ·

Learn three clean jokes.

· 22 ·

Wear polished shoes.

· 23 ·

Floss your teeth.

· 24 ·

Drink champagne for no reason at all.

· 25 ·

Ask for a raise when you feel you've earned it.

· 26 ·

If in a fight, hit first and hit hard.

· 27 ·

Return all things you borrow.

· 28 ·

Teach some kind of class.

· 29 ·

Be a student in some kind of class.

· 30 ·

Never buy a house without a fireplace.

· 31 ·

Buy whatever kids are selling
on card tables in their front yards.

· 32 ·

Once in your life own a convertible.

· 33 ·

Treat everyone you meet like you want
to be treated.

· 34 ·

Learn to identify the music
of Chopin, Mozart, and Beethoven.

· 35 ·

Plant a tree on your birthday.

· 36 ·

Donate two pints of blood every year.

· 37 ·

Make new friends but cherish the old ones.

· 38 ·

Keep secrets.

· 39 ·

Take lots of snapshots.

· 40 ·

Never refuse homemade brownies.

· 41 ·

Don't postpone joy.

· 42 ·

Write "thank you" notes promptly.

· 43 ·

Never give up
on anybody.
Miracles happen every day.

· 44 ·

Show respect for teachers.

· 45 ·

Show respect for police officers and firefighters.

· 46 ·

Show respect for military personnel.

· 47 ·

Don't waste time
learning the "tricks of the trade."
Instead, learn the trade.

· 48 ·

Keep a tight rein on your temper.

· 49 ·

Buy vegetables from truck farmers
who advertise with hand-lettered signs.

· 50 ·

Put the cap back on the toothpaste.

· 51 ·

Take out the garbage without being told.

· 52 ·

Avoid overexposure to the sun.

· 53 ·

Vote.

· 54 ·

Surprise loved ones with little unexpected gifts.

· 55 ·

Stop blaming others. Take responsibility
for every area of your life.

· 56 ·

Never mention being on a diet.

· 57 ·

Make the best of bad situations.

· 58 ·

Always accept an outstretched hand.

· 59 ·

Live so that when your children think of fairness,
caring, and integrity, they think of you.

· 60 ·

Admit your mistakes.

· 61 ·

Ask someone to pick up your mail and
daily paper when you're out of town. Those are
the first two things potential burglars look for.

· 62 ·

Use your wit to amuse, not abuse.

· 63 ·

Remember that all news is biased.

· 64 ·

Take a photography course.

· 65 ·

Let people pull in front of you
when you're stopped in traffic.

· 66 ·

Support a high school band.

· 67 ·

Demand excellence and be willing to pay for it.

· 68 ·

Be brave.
Even if you're not,
pretend to be.
No one can tell
the difference.

· 69 ·

Whistle.

· 70 ·

Hug children after you discipline them.

· 71 ·

Learn to make something beautiful
with your hands.

· 72 ·

Give to charity all the clothes you
haven't worn during the past three years.

· 73 ·

Never forget your anniversary.

· 74 ·

Eat prunes.

· 75 ·

Ride a bike.

· 76 ·

Choose a charity in your community
and support it generously with
your time and money.

· 77 ·

Don't take good health for granted.

· 78 ·

When someone wants to hire you,
even if it's for a job you have little interest in,
talk to them. Never close the door on
an opportunity until you've had a chance
to hear the offer in person.

· 79 ·

Don't mess with drugs, and don't
associate with those who do.

· 80 ·

Slow dance.

· 81 ·

Avoid sarcastic remarks.

· 82 ·

Steer clear of restaurants
with strolling musicians.

· 83 ·

In business and in family relationships,
remember that the most important thing is trust.

· 84 ·

Forget the Joneses.

· 85 ·

Never encourage anyone to become a lawyer.

· 86 ·

Don't smoke.

· 87 ·

Even if you're financially well-to-do,
have your children earn and pay
part of their college tuition.

· 88 ·

Even if you're financially well-to-do,
have your children earn and pay
for *all* their automobile insurance.

· 89 ·

Recycle old newspapers, bottles, and cans.

· 90 ·

Refill ice cube trays.

· 91 ·

Don't let anyone ever see you tipsy.

· 92 ·

Never invest more in the stock market
than you can afford to lose.

· 93 ·

Choose your life's mate carefully.
From this one decision will come ninety percent
of all your happiness or misery.

· 94 ·

Make it a habit to do nice things
for people who'll never find it out.

· 95 ·

Attend class reunions.

· 96 ·

Lend only those books
you never care to see again.

· 97 ·

Always have something beautiful in sight,
even if it's just a daisy in a jelly glass.

· 98 ·

Know how to type.

· 99 ·

Think big thoughts, but relish small pleasures.

· 100 ·

Read the Bill of Rights.

· 101 ·

Learn how to read a financial report.

· 102 ·

Tell your kids often how terrific they are
and that you trust them.

· 103 ·

Use credit cards only for convenience,
never for credit.

· 104 ·

Take a brisk thirty-minute walk every day.

· 105 ·

Treat yourself to a massage on your birthday.

· 106 ·

Never cheat.

· 107 ·

Smile a lot. It costs nothing
and is beyond price.

· 108 ·

When dining with clients or business associates,
never order more than one cocktail or one
glass of wine. If no one else is drinking,
don't drink at all.

· 109 ·

Know how to drive a stick shift.

· 110 ·

Spread crunchy peanut butter
on Pepperidge Farm Gingerman cookies
for the perfect late-night snack.

· 111 ·

Never use profanity.

· 112 ·

Never argue with police officers,
and address them as "officer."

· 113 ·

Learn to identify local
wildflowers, birds, and trees.

· 114 ·

Keep a fire extinguisher in your kitchen and car.

· 115 ·

Give yourself a year
and read the Bible cover to cover.

· 116 ·

Consider writing a living will.

· 117 ·

Install dead bolt locks on outside doors.

· 118 ·

Don't buy expensive wine, luggage, or watches.

· 119 ·

Put a lot of little marshmallows
in your hot chocolate.

· 120 ·

Learn CPR.

· 121 ·

Resist the temptation to buy a boat.

· 122 ·

Stop and read historical roadside markers.

· 123 ·

Learn to listen. Opportunity sometimes knocks very softly.

· 124 ·

Know how to change a tire.

· 125 ·

Know how to tie a bow tie.

· 126 ·

Respect your children's privacy.
Knock before entering their room.

· 127 ·

Wear audacious underwear
under the most solemn business attire.

· 128 ·

Remember people's names.

· 129 ·

Introduce yourself to the manager
where you bank. It's important that
he/she knows you personally.

· 130 ·

Leave the toilet seat in the down position.

· 131 ·

Learn the capitals of the states.

· 132 ·

Visit Washington, D.C., and do the tourist bit.

· 133 ·

When someone is relating an important
event that's happened to them, don't try
to top them with a story of your own.
Let them have the stage.

· 134 ·

Don't buy cheap tools.
Craftsman tools from Sears are among the best.

· 135 ·

Have crooked teeth straightened.

· 136 ·

Have dull-colored teeth whitened.

· 137 ·

Keep your watch five minutes fast.

· 138 ·

Learn Spanish. In a few years,
more than thirty-five percent of all Americans
will speak it as their first language.

· 139 ·

Never deprive someone of hope; it might be all they have.

· 140 ·

When starting out, don't worry about
not having enough money.
Limited funds are a blessing,
not a curse. Nothing encourages creative
thinking in quite the same way.

· 141 ·

Give yourself an hour to cool off before
responding to someone who has provoked you.
If it involves something really important,
give yourself overnight.

· 142 ·

Pay your bills on time.

· 143 ·

Join a slow-pitch softball league.

· 144 ·

Take someone bowling.

· 145 ·

Keep a flashlight and extra batteries
under the bed and in the glove box of your car.

· 146 ·

When playing games with children, let them win.

· 147 ·

Turn off the television at dinner time.

· 148 ·

Learn to handle a pistol and rifle safely.

· 149 ·

Skip one meal a week and give
what you would have spent to a street person.

· 150 ·

Sing in a choir.

· 151 ·

Get acquainted with a good
lawyer, accountant, and plumber.

· 152 ·

Fly Old Glory on the Fourth of July.

· 153 ·

Stand at attention and put your hand over
your heart when singing the national anthem.

· 154 ·

Resist the temptation to put a cute message
on your answering machine.

· 155 ·

Have a will and tell your next-of-kin where it is.

· 156 ·

Strive for excellence, not perfection.

· 157 ·

Take time to smell the roses.

· 158 ·

Pray not for things,
but for wisdom and courage.

· 159 ·

Be tough minded but tenderhearted.

· 160 ·

Use seat belts.

· 161 ·

Have regular medical and dental checkups.

· 162 ·

Keep your desk and work area neat.

· 163 ·

Take an overnight train trip
and sleep in a Pullman.

· 164 ·

Be punctual and insist on it in others.

· 165 ·

Don't waste time responding to your critics.

· 166 ·

Avoid negative people.

· 167 ·

Don't scrimp in order to
leave money to your children.

· 168 ·

Resist telling people how something should be
done. Instead, tell them *what* needs to be done.
They will often surprise you
with creative solutions.

· 169 ·

Be original.

· 170 ·

Be neat.

· 171 ·

Never give up on what you really want to do.
The person with big dreams is more powerful
than one with all the facts.

· 172 ·

Be suspicious of all politicians.

· 173 ·

Be kinder than necessary.

· 174 ·

Encourage your children to have
a part-time job after the age of sixteen.

· 175 ·

Give people a second chance, but not a third.

· 176 ·

Read carefully anything
that requires your signature.
Remember the big print giveth
and the small print taketh away.

· 177 ·

Never take action when you're angry.

· 178 ·

Learn to recognize the inconsequential,
then ignore it.

· 179 ·

Be your wife's best friend.

· 180 ·

Do battle against prejudice and discrimination
wherever you find it.

· 181 ·

Wear out, don't rust out.

· 182 ·

Be romantic.

· 183 ·

Let people know what you stand for—
and what you won't stand for.

· 184 ·

Don't quit a job
until you've lined up another.

· 185 ·

Never criticize the person
who signs your paycheck.
If you are unhappy with your job, resign.

· 186 ·

Be insatiably curious.
Ask "why" a lot.

· 187 ·

Measure people by the size of their hearts,
not the size of their bank accounts.

· 188 ·

Become the most positive and enthusiastic person you know.

· 189 ·

Learn how to fix a leaky faucet and toilet.

· 190 ·

Have good posture.
Enter a room with purpose
and confidence.

· 191 ·

Don't worry that you can't
give your kids the best of everything.
Give them *your* very best.

· 192 ·

Drink low fat milk.

· 193 ·

Use less salt.

· 194 ·

Eat less red meat.

· 195 ·

Determine the quality of a neighborhood
by the manners of the people living there.

· 196 ·

Surprise a new neighbor
with one of your favorite homemade dishes
—and include the recipe.

· 197 ·

Don't forget,
a person's greatest emotional need
is to feel appreciated.

· 198 ·

Feed a stranger's expired parking meter.

· 199 ·

Park at the back of the lot at shopping centers.
The walk is good exercise.

· 200 ·

Don't watch violent television shows,
and don't buy the products that sponsor them.

· 201 ·

Don't carry a grudge.

· 202 ·

Show respect for all living things.

· 203 ·

Return borrowed vehicles
with the gas tank full.

· 204 ·

Choose work that is
in harmony with your values.

· 205 ·

Loosen up. Relax. Except for
rare life-and-death matters, nothing
is as important as it first seems.

· 206 ·

Give your best to your employer.
It's one of the best investments you can make.

· 207 ·

Swing for the fence.

· 208 ·

Attend high school art shows,
and always buy something.

· 209 ·

Observe the speed limit.

· 210 ·

Commit yourself to constant self-improvement.

· 211 ·

Take your dog to obedience school.
You'll both learn a lot.

· 212 ·

Don't allow the phone
to interrupt important moments.
It's there for your convenience, not the caller's.

· 213 ·

Don't waste time grieving over past mistakes.
Learn from them and move on.

· 214 ·

When complimented, a sincere "thank you"
is the only response required.

· 215 ·

Don't plan a long evening on a blind date.
A lunch date is perfect. If things don't work out,
both of you have only wasted an hour.

· 216 ·

Don't discuss business in elevators.
You never know who may overhear you.

· 217 ·

Be a good loser.

· 218 ·

Be a good winner.

· 219 ·

Never go grocery shopping when you're hungry.
You'll buy too much.

· 220 ·

Spend less time worrying *who's* right,
and more time deciding *what's* right.

· 221 ·

Don't major
in minor things.

· 222 ·

Think twice before burdening
a friend with a secret.

· 223 ·

Praise in public.

· 224 ·

Criticize in private.

· 225 ·

Never tell anyone they look tired or depressed.

· 226 ·

When someone hugs you,
let them be the first to let go.

· 227 ·

Resist giving advice concerning,
matrimony, finances, or hair styles.

· 228 ·

Have impeccable manners.

· 229 ·

Never pay for work before it's completed.

· 230 ·

Keep good company.

· 231 ·

Keep a daily journal.

· 232 ·

Keep your promises.

· 233 ·

Avoid any church that has cushions on the pews
and is considering building a gymnasium.

· 234 ·

Teach your children the value of money
and the importance of saving.

· 235 ·

Be willing to lose a battle
in order to win the war.

· 236 ·

Don't be deceived by first impressions.

· 237 ·

Seek out the good in people.

· 238 ·

Don't encourage rude or inattentive service
by tipping the standard amount.

· 239 ·

Watch the movie
It's A Wonderful Life every Christmas.

· 240 ·

Drink eight glasses of water every day.

· 241 ·

Respect tradition.

· 242 ·

Be cautious about lending money to friends.
You might lose both.

· 243 ·

Never waste an opportunity
to tell good employees how much
they mean to the company.

· 244 ·

Buy a bird feeder and hang it so that
you can see it from your kitchen window.

· 245 ·

Never cut
what can be untied.

· 246 ·

Wave at children on school buses.

· 247 ·

Tape record your parents' memories
of how they met and their first
years of marriage.

· 248 ·

Show respect for others' time.
Call whenever you're going to be more
than ten minutes late for an appointment.

· 249 ·

Hire people smarter than you.

· 250 ·

Learn to show cheerfulness,
even when you don't feel like it.

· 251 ·

Learn to show enthusiasm,
even when you don't feel like it.

· 252 ·

Take good care of those you love.

· 253 ·

Be modest. A lot
was accomplished before you were born.

· 254 ·

Keep it simple.

· 255 ·

Purchase gas from the neighborhood gas station
even if it costs more. Next winter when
it's six degrees and your car won't start,
you'll be glad they know you.

· 256 ·

Don't jaywalk.

· 257 ·

Never ask a lawyer or accountant
for business advice. They are trained
to find problems, not solutions.

· 258 ·

When meeting someone for the first time,
resist asking what they do for a living.
Enjoy their company without attaching any labels.

· 259 ·

Avoid like the plague any lawsuit.

· 260 ·

Every day show your family how much
you love them with your words, with your touch,
and with your thoughtfulness.

· 261 ·

Take family vacations
whether you can afford them or not.
The memories will be priceless.

· 262 ·

Don't gossip.

· 263 ·

Don't discuss salaries.

· 264 ·

Don't nag.

· 265 ·

Don't gamble.

· 266 ·

Beware of the person who has nothing to lose.

· 267 ·

Lie on your back and look at the stars.

· 268 ·

Don't leave car keys in the ignition.

· 269 ·

Don't whine.

· 270 ·

Arrive at work early
and stay beyond quitting time.

· 271 ·

When facing a difficult task,
act as though it is impossible to fail.
If you're going after Moby Dick,
take along the tarter sauce.

· 272 ·

Change air conditioner filters
every three months.

· 273 ·

Remember that overnight success
usually takes about fifteen years.

· 274 ·

Leave everything
a little better
than you found it.

· 275 ·

Cut out complimentary newspaper articles
about people you know and mail the
articles to them with notes of congratulations.

· 276 ·

Patronize local merchants
even if it costs a bit more.

· 277 ·

Fill your gas tank when it
falls below one-quarter full.

· 278 ·

Don't expect money to bring you happiness.

· 279 ·

Never snap your fingers
to get someone's attention. It's rude.

· 280 ·

No matter how dire the situation,
keep your cool.

· 281 ·

When paying cash, ask for a discount.

· 282 ·

Find a good tailor.

· 283 ·

Don't use a toothpick in public.

· 284 ·

Never underestimate
your power to change yourself.

· 285 ·

Never overestimate
your power to change others.

· 286 ·

Practice empathy. Try to see things
from other people's point of view.

· 287 ·

Promise big. Deliver big.

· 288 ·

Discipline yourself to save money.
It's essential to success.

· 289 ·

Get and stay in shape.

· 290 ·

Find some other way of proving
your manhood than by shooting
defenseless animals and birds.

· 291 ·

Remember the deal's not done
until the check has cleared the bank.

· 292 ·

Don't burn bridges.
You'll be surprised how many times
you have to cross the same river.

· 293 ·

Don't spread yourself too thin.
Learn to say *no* politely and quickly.

· 294 ·

Keep overhead low.

· 295 ·

Keep expectations high.

· 296 ·

Accept pain and disappointment as part of life.

· 297 ·

Remember that a successful marriage depends
on two things: (1) finding the right person
and (2) being the right person.

· 298 ·

See problems as opportunities
for growth and self-mastery.

· 299 ·

Don't believe people when they
ask you to be honest with them.

· 300 ·

Don't expect life to be fair.

· 301 ·

Become an expert in time management.

· 302 ·

Lock your car even if it's
parked in your own driveway.

· 303 ·

Never go to bed with dirty dishes in the sink.

· 304 ·

Judge your success
by the degree
that you're enjoying
peace, health, and love.

· 305 ·

Learn to handle a handsaw and a hammer.

· 306 ·

Take a nap on Sunday afternoons.

· 307 ·

Compliment the meal when you're
a guest in someone's home.

· 308 ·

Make the bed when you're
an overnight visitor in someone's home.

· 309 ·

Contribute five percent of your income
to charity.

· 310 ·

Don't leave a ring in the bathtub.

· 311 ·

Don't waste time playing cards.

· 312 ·

When tempted to criticize your parents,
spouse, or children, bite your tongue.

· 313 ·

Never underestimate the power of love.

· 314 ·

Never underestimate the power of forgiveness.

· 315 ·

Don't bore people with your problems.
When someone asks you how you feel
—say, "Terrific, never better." When
they ask, "How's business?" reply,
"Excellent, and getting better every day."

· 316 ·

Learn to disagree
without being disagreeable.

· 317 ·

Be tactful. Never alienate anyone on purpose.

· 318 ·

Hear both sides before judging.

· 319 ·

Refrain from envy.
It's the source of much unhappiness.

· 320 ·

Be courteous to everyone.

· 321 ·

Wave to crosswalk patrol mothers.

· 322 ·

Don't say you don't have enough time.
You have exactly the same number of hours per
day that were given to Pasteur, Michaelangelo,
Mother Teresa, Helen Keller, Leonardo da Vinci,
Thomas Jefferson, and Albert Einstein.

· 323 ·

When there's no time
for a full work-out, do push-ups.

· 324 ·

Don't delay acting on a good idea. Chances
are someone else has just thought of it, too.
Success comes to the one who acts first.

· 325 ·

Be wary of people who tell you
how honest they are.

· 326 ·

Remember that winners do
what losers don't want to do.

· 327 ·

When you arrive at your job in the morning,
let the first thing you say brighten everyone's day.

· 328 ·

Seek opportunity, not security.
A boat in a harbor is safe, but
in time its bottom will rot out.

· 329 ·

Install smoke detectors in your home.

· 330 ·

Rekindle old friendships.

· 331 ·

When traveling, put a card in your wallet
with your name, home phone, the phone
number of a friend or close relative, important
medical information, plus the phone number
of the hotel or motel where you're staying.

· 332 ·

Live your life as an exclamation, not an explanation.

· 333 ·

Instead of using the words, *if only*,
try substituting the words, *next time*.

· 334 ·

Instead of using the word *problem*,
try substituting the word *opportunity*.

· 335 ·

Ever so often push your luck.

· 336 ·

Get your next pet from the animal shelter.

· 337 ·

Reread your favorite book.

· 338 ·

Live your life so that your
epitaph could read, "No regrets."

· 339 ·

Never walk out on a quarrel with your wife.

· 340 ·

Don't think a higher price
always means higher quality.

· 341 ·

Don't be fooled. If something sounds
too good to be true, it probably is.

· 342 ·

When renting a car for a couple of days,
splurge and get the big Lincoln.

· 343 ·

Regarding furniture and clothes:
if you think you'll be using them five years
or longer, buy the best you can afford.

· 344 ·

Patronize drug stores with soda fountains.

· 345 ·

Try everything offered
by supermarket food demonstrators.

· 346 ·

Be bold and courageous.
When you look back on your life,
you'll regret the things you didn't do
more than the ones you did.

· 347 ·

Never waste an opportunity to tell someone you love them.

· 348 ·

Own a good dictionary.

· 349 ·

Own a good thesaurus.

· 350 ·

Remember the three most important things
when buying a home: location, location, location.

· 351 ·

Keep valuable papers in a bank lockbox.

· 352 ·

Just for fun, attend a small town
Fourth of July celebration.

· 353 ·

Go through all your old photographs.
Select ten and tape them to your kitchen
cabinets. Change them every thirty days.

· 354 ·

To explain a romantic break-up,
simply say, "It was all my fault."

· 355 ·

Evaluate yourself by your own standards,
not someone else's.

· 356 ·

Be there when people need you.

· 357 ·

Let your representatives in Washington know
how you feel. Call (202) 225-3121 for the House
and (202) 224-3121 for the Senate. An operator
will connect you to the right office.

· 358 ·

Be decisive even if it means
you'll sometimes be wrong.

· 359 ·

Don't let anyone talk you out of pursuing
what you know to be a great idea.

· 360 ·

Be prepared to lose once in a while.

· 361 ·

Never eat the last cookie.

· 362 ·

Know when to keep silent.

· 363 ·

Know when to speak up.

· 364 ·

Every day look for some small way
to improve your marriage.

· 365 ·

Every day look for some small way
to improve the way you do your job.

· 366 ·

Don't flush urinals with
your hand—use your elbow.

· 367 ·

Acquire things the old-fashioned way:
Save for them and pay cash.

· 368 ·

Remember no one makes it alone.
Have a grateful heart and be quick
to acknowledge those who help you.

· 369 ·

Read *Leadership is an Art* by Max DePree
(Dell, 1989).

· 370 ·

Do business with those
who do business with you.

· 371 ·

Just to see how it feels,
for the next twenty-four hours refrain
from criticizing anybody or anything.

· 372 ·

Give your clients your enthusiastic best.

· 373 ·

Let your children overhear
you saying complimentary things
about them to other adults.

· 374 ·

Work hard to create in your children a
good self-image. It's the most important thing
you can do to insure their success.

· 375 ·

Take charge
of your attitude.
Don't let someone else
choose it for you.

· 376 ·

Save an evening a week
for just you and your wife.

· 377 ·

Carry jumper cables in your car.

· 378 ·

Get all repair estimates in writing.

· 379 ·

Forget committees. New, noble,
world-changing ideas always come
from one person working alone.

· 380 ·

Pay attention to the details.

· 381 ·

Be a self-starter.

· 382 ·

Be loyal.

· 383 ·

Understand that happiness is not based on
possessions, power, or prestige, but on
relationships with people you love and respect.

· 384 ·

Never give a loved one a gift
that suggests they need improvement.

· 385 ·

Compliment even small improvements.

· 386 ·

Turn off the tap when brushing your teeth.

· 387 ·

Wear expensive shoes, belts, and ties,
but buy them on sale.

· 388 ·

When undecided about what color
to paint a room, choose antique white.

· 389 ·

Carry stamps in your wallet.
You never know when you'll discover
the perfect card for a friend or loved one.

· 390 ·

Street musicians are a treasure.
Stop for a moment and listen;
then leave a small donation.

· 391 ·

Support equal pay for equal work.

· 392 ·

Pay your fair share.

· 393 ·

Learn how to operate a Macintosh computer.

· 394 ·

When faced with a serious health problem,
get at least three medical opinions.

· 395 ·

Remain open, flexible, curious.

· 396 ·

Never give anyone a fruitcake.

· 397 ·

Never acquire just one kitten.
Two are a lot more fun and no more trouble.

· 398 ·

Start meetings on time
regardless of who's missing.

· 399 ·

Focus on making things better, not bigger.

· 400 ·

Stay out of nightclubs.

· 401 ·

Don't ever watch hot dogs
or sausage being made.

· 402 ·

Begin each day with your favorite music.

· 403 ·

Visit your city's night court on a Saturday night.

· 404 ·

When attending meetings, sit down front.

· 405 ·

Don't be intimidated by doctors and nurses.
Even when you're in the hospital,
it's still your body.

· 406 ·

Read hospital bills carefully.
It's reported that 89% contain errors
—in favor of the hospital.

· 407 ·

Every once in a while, take the scenic route.

· 408 ·

Don't let your possessions possess you.

· 409 ·

Wage war against littering.

· 410 ·

Send a lot of Valentine cards.
Sign them, "Someone who thinks you're terrific."

· 411 ·

Cut your own firewood.

· 412 ·

When you and your wife have a disagreement,
regardless of who's wrong, apologize. Say,
"I'm sorry I upset you. Would you forgive me?"
These are healing, magical words.

· 413 ·

Don't flaunt your success,
but don't apologize for it either.

· 414 ·

After experiencing inferior service, food,
or products, bring it to the attention
of the person in charge. Good managers
will appreciate knowing.

· 415 ·

Be enthusiastic about the success of others.

· 416 ·

Don't procrastinate. Do what needs
doing when it needs to be done.

· 417 ·

Read to your children.

· 418 ·

Sing to your children.

· 419 ·

Listen to your children.

· 420 ·

Get your priorities straight.
No one ever said on his death bed,
"Gee, if I'd only spent more time at the office."

· 421 ·

Take care
of your reputation.
It's your
most valuable asset.

· 422 ·

Turn on your headlights when it begins to rain.

· 423 ·

Don't tailgate.

· 424 ·

Sign and carry your organ donor card.

· 425 ·

Don't allow self-pity. The moment
this emotion strikes, do something nice
for someone less fortunate than you.

· 426 ·

Share the credit.

· 427 ·

Don't accept "good enough" as good enough.

· 428 ·

Do more than is expected.

· 429 ·

Go to a county fair and
check out the 4-H Club exhibits.
It will renew your faith in the younger generation.

· 430 ·

Select a doctor your own age
so that you can grow old together.

· 431 ·

Use club soda as an emergency spot remover.

· 432 ·

Improve your performance
by improving your attitude.

· 433 ·

Have a friend who owns a truck.

· 434 ·

At the movies, buy Junior Mints
and sprinkle them on your popcorn.

· 435 ·

Make a list of twenty-five things you
want to experience before you die.
Carry it in your wallet and refer to it often.

· 436 ·

Have some knowledge of three religions
other than your own.

· 437 ·

Answer the phone with enthusiasm
and energy in your voice.

· 438 ·

Every person that you meet knows
something you don't; learn from them.

· 439 ·

Tape record your parents' laughter.

· 440 ·

Buy cars that have air bags.

· 441 ·

When meeting someone you don't know well,
extend your hand and give them your name.
Never assume they remember you
even if you've met them before.

· 442 ·

Do it right the first time.

· 443 ·

Laugh a lot.
A good sense of humor cures
almost all of life's ills.

· 444 ·

Never underestimate
the power
of a kind word or deed.

· 445 ·

Don't undertip the waiter just because
the food is bad; he didn't cook it.

· 446 ·

Change your car's oil and filter every
three thousand miles regardless of what
the owner's manual recommends.

· 447 ·

Conduct family fire drills.
Be sure everyone knows what to do
in case the house catches fire.

· 448 ·

Don't be afraid to say, "I don't know."

· 449 ·

Don't be afraid to say, "I made a mistake."

· 450 ·

Don't be afraid to say, "I need help."

· 451 ·

Don't be afraid to say, "I'm sorry."

· 452 ·

Never compromise your integrity.

· 453 ·

Keep a note pad and pencil
on your bedside table.
Million-dollar ideas sometimes strike at 3 A.M.

· 454 ·

Show respect for everyone who works for a living,
regardless of how trivial their job.

· 455 ·

Read the Sunday *New York Times*
to keep informed.

· 456 ·

Send your loved one flowers.
Think of a reason later.

· 457 ·

Attend your children's
athletic contests, plays, and recitals.

· 458 ·

When you find a job that's ideal,
take it regardless of the pay. If you've got
what it takes, your salary will soon reflect
your value to the company.

· 459 ·

Don't use time or words carelessly.
Neither can be retrieved.

· 460 ·

Look for opportunities
to make people feel important.

· 461 ·

Get organized. If you don't know
where to start, read Stephanie Winston's
Getting Organized (Warner Books, 1978).

· 462 ·

When a child falls and skins a knee or elbow,
always show concern; then take the time
to "kiss it and make it well."

· 463 ·

Be open to new ideas.

· 464 ·

Don't miss the magic of the moment
by focusing on what's to come.

· 465 ·

When talking to the press, remember
they always have the last word.

· 466 ·

Set short-term and long-term goals.

· 467 ·

When planning a trip abroad,
read about the places you'll visit before you go
or, better yet, rent a travel video.

· 468 ·

Don't rain on other people's parades.

· 469 ·

Stand when greeting a visitor to your office.

· 470 ·

Don't interrupt.

· 471 ·

Before leaving to meet a flight,
call the airline first to be sure it's on time.

· 472 ·

Enjoy real maple syrup.

· 473 ·

Don't be rushed into making an important
decision. People will understand if you say,
"I'd like a little more time to think it over.
Can I get back to you tomorrow?"

· 474 ·

Be prepared. You never get
a second chance to make
a good first impression.

· 475 ·

Don't expect others to listen to your advice
and ignore your example.

· 476 ·

Go the distance.
When you accept a task, finish it.

· 477 ·

Give thanks before every meal.

· 478 ·

Don't insist on running someone else's life.

· 479 ·

Respond promptly to R.S.V.P. invitations.
If there's a phone number, call;
if not, write a note.

· 480 ·

Take a kid to the zoo.

· 481 ·

Watch for big problems. They disguise big opportunities.

· 482 ·

Get into the habit
of putting your billfold and car keys
in the same place when entering your home.

· 483 ·

Learn a card trick.

· 484 ·

Steer clear of restaurants that rotate.

· 485 ·

Give people the benefit of the doubt.

· 486 ·

Never admit at work
that you're tired, angry, or bored.

· 487 ·

Decide to get up thirty minutes earlier.
Do this for a year, and you will add
seven and one-half days to your waking world.

· 488 ·

Make someone's day by paying the toll
for the person in the car behind you.

· 489 ·

Don't make the same mistake twice.

· 490 ·

Don't drive on slick tires.

· 491 ·

Keep an extra key hidden somewhere
on your car in case you lock yourself out.

· 492 ·

Put an insulation blanket around your
hot water heater to conserve energy.

· 493 ·

Save ten percent of what you earn.

· 494 ·

Never discuss money with people
who have much more or much less than you.

· 495 ·

Never buy a beige car.

· 496 ·

Never buy something you don't need
just because it's on sale.

· 497 ·

Don't be called out on strikes. Go down swinging.

· 498 ·

Question your goals by asking,
"Will this help me become my very best?"

· 499 ·

Cherish your children for what they are,
not for what you'd like them to be.

· 500 ·

When negotiating your salary,
think of what you want; then ask
for ten percent more.

· 501 ·

Keep several irons in the fire.

· 502 ·

After you've worked hard to get what you want,
take the time to enjoy it.

· 503 ·

Be alert for opportunities
to show praise and appreciation.

· 504 ·

Commit yourself to quality.

· 505 ·

Be a leader:
Remember the lead sled dog
is the only one with a decent view.

· 506 ·

Never underestimate the power of words
to heal and reconcile relationships.

· 507 ·

Your mind can only hold one thought at a time.
Make it a positive and constructive one.

· 508 ·

Become someone's hero.

· 509 ·

Marry only for love.

· 510 ·

Count your blessings.

· 511 ·

Call your mother.